As a child, I asked for a typewriter for my 10th birthday. I would slowly take the hard case off of the old Underwood everyday in an act of ceremony. It became a sacred technology, something that held while transmuting thoughts otherwise beyond my capacity to articulate. An oracle. A talisman. It is where lyric found me. Cat Chong's Dear Lettera 32 has this same divining quality. It sucks me in, and I feel transported by the textural language in its disrupting yet comforting familiarity. It is ever-changing, mobile. It asks me to be languidly alert, brilliantly read through the body in all its limits and possibilities "with magic and the poem" pressed up against it, "cast in subdermal frequencies". It makes me want to learn to write again, to be "witness to vulnerability with every mark."

Cassandra Troyan

In their conversation with JD Howse, Cat Chong asks if Dear Lettera 32 reads like a retaliation. But here, left to their own device - the typewriter - the poet writes themselves through, into, and out of microaggressions, crip theory, citation, and embodiment, in a crushing juxtaposition of density and blankness. And in this breath-denial and linelessness, the text asks how it could become a form of accountability; how do we hold people to account? How do we give an account of ourselves? Throughout the compressed orientations of the prose poems, dreams recur as relationality, violence, a kind of consciousness, and a possible alternate space of escape. In this multiplicity, turning away and back towards the realness of poetry, Chong writes a will to go on, go on, go on; to hope.

Prudence Bussey-Chamberlain

In beginning Cat Chong's Dear Lettera 32 the reader must straight away bend under the weight of the typewriter, learning the bunch and give of each page as crowded text gives way to blank space. This book is mired in isolation, reaching out in its intertextuality to avoid any individual voice to dominate, always in conversation and perhaps most of all when lonely. Chong begins one letter 'I am accumulating. text': text which reads both as curse and blessing, trauma and hex, envying the 'ability to say nothing'. The speaker accuses and pleads with their subject/s, unspooling and unsure of the poem's own nature, claiming 'no desire to resemble', nonetheless – or perhaps accordingly – capable of illuminating and spitting on the hostile power structures bearing down here and everywhere. This is vital work.

Kat Sinclair

Dear Lettera 32
by Cat Chong

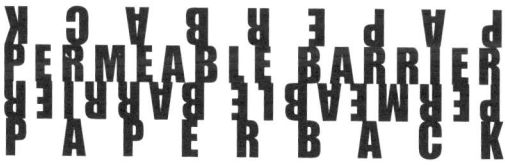

PERMEABLE BARRIER PAPERBACK

Dear Lettera 32

Dear Lettera 32
              / elegaic love. letters. the typewriter

Dear Lettera 32
              / part i

Dear Lettera 32,

howmuchforceisrequiredtomoveforward to cross across. the
page a measurement of distance a haunt.ink mess this
constant. curling here. my vocabulary is a necessity of
compression along straight lines.all maintaining. parallels.
a leaf fell off the lime tree while you were gone. maybe
this. a language as a type of force fuck maybe this is
what the blonde poets knew about. there's something
wonderful about. the mechanism about being. an idealised
pacifist about putting Trump to death slowly with nasal
surgery pillow talk. i think turpitude sounds better when
you say it out loud. like watching paper straighten in
the afternoon humidity this makes me. care-less about
mistakes I am making word.marks out of meaning and metal.
it is not silent. in this Singapore a terminal velocity
its looking for examples to be made out. of you and me
in these are small times of keeping. I know you. will
not stay forever that there will be a goodbye hope. your
leaving will not be quiet hope I will miss you every day
I will miss you

Dear Lettera 32,

is this a poem that I'm writing for you? leaving language
where I can see it where. is the paper going? reach
inside and touch the ink with my fingers all this an
analogue of machine parts the ink arc red and black tape
this density and convoluting I wish you would always be.
within two minutes of distance how will I get the paper
out? slowly turning backwards falling out is the
opposite circulation you make. the best pancakes I feel
safer knowing that you're here your eyes are so startlingly
blue you're into trouble in my nightmares sorrow and
rage are appropriate Ariana Reines May 19 5:05am I know
I'm probably saying it wrong. we have a human debt of
solidarity. I don't want to make my success successes
unforgivable designate your bookshelves a place of
worship to see you again a part of poet family of
language instead of blood this strange accretion of
speech

Dear Lettera 32,

I am mutable leaving this space for less than 3 hours
a week waiting on the surface of this secret. machine
for ending something that I'm hiding the poem. a
suspension space somewhere to go for renewal you're
the only one. i've seen. you're the only one in my
dreams how writing this way means I can never see the
line that came before the poem becomes part of the
surprise. You want to fuck with it don't you?"---yes
--yes--yes is dropping or being dropped one by one lost
spaces containing everything I am dropping all the
bowlsmugscupssaucersglasses I don't remember how the
poem started something untraceable maybe on an
extraverbal level hope. can you feel me these small
aggregates each one a deep secret something crepuscular
like depth or twilight to Broc Norman Rossell to this.
typewriter you lent me to these months of silence words
with nowhere else to go eye give my Is over to rest
no longer able to hold. them apart it is dawn and I
have not slept for three months I've had the moon in my
eyes I know I could tell the different shades of the
sky at night just before dawn all this red light rising

Dear Lettera 32,
I am writing on the back. of spare paper NAME OF LIFE
TO BE INSURED for this reassurance please turn. over I
will be. ok please just turn. over and go back. to sleep

Dear Lettera 32,

I have seen you so my nightmares say that you'll kill
me. with both your hands it's getting hard to hide. how
tired I am if I am. awake I am writing to you and the
possibility of sleep to sing myself away and give
myself over I think I can't give anyone anything whoever
it is I wish I could remember my body. spills over holding.
together something I don't know how to name. anyone
anymore. I am always writing. my way out but more and
more I am writing to be. some-place closer to you in
my work the way is frequently associated with departure
I welcome this new relationship with a kind of arrival

Dear Lettera 32,
how are you? I feel like an immensity

Dear Lettera 32,

I am still thinking about death an aortic aneurism
blood in the space where space should be legs and feet
blistering from newly acquired lack to enter. feet first
walking into it without saying goodbye with only
momentum and no way out I think you will always be there
in those rooms where he turns wood and bone you have a
voice like liquid silk "I've said my prayer I'm not
gonna pontificate" Ariana Reines June 2 she is right
when she says everything is on fire "the construction
of white innocence indeed" Ariana Reines June 4 to have
my hair cut is to lose what I want to be lost and
at the same time to be touched again

Dear Lettera 32,

I have never been. awake for so many sunrises my eyes
are all the way open is poetry like this dreaming for a
new kind of consciousness I wish it would stop-the
nerve of my eye-to just keep twitching. I wish all over.
again to scroll backwards up the page is to fly backwards
in time to recall your blue eyes smiling the birds. are
calling out and it is dawn again I try screaming behind
the reusable cloth mask I make as much sound as a whimper
I accidentally cut my tongue licking a craft knife in
the mirror. I stare at the owner of my face and watch
it bleed an image of self-consumption. the poem an act
of salvage a kind of treachery into unsafe language.I am
still writing in. hope survival to type on a typewriter
is to make the poem an extended uncurling with each
punched in letter reading the outline behind the impression
of the last a poetry of continuous indentation staring at
the page as it rolls back into obscurity

Dear Lettera 32,

being awake is exhausting there are so many ways in which
I would rather just sleep for many hours on end till
I could call myself a longitude this is obviously a
metaphor for a kind of hanging up like the telephone
or a pole a type of alignment this way or that in which
I have a decent idea as to how many directions there
are at the start I am writing on this another scrap
the back of a financial keeping does that make this a
statement or another kind of steamrolling I'm never
entirely sure what to do with my weight my altered
sense of gravity I should go back to sleep maybe this
is all just a way to get back there for another few
impermanent hours

Dear Lettera 32,
at 9:30pm I exit my room to see small red ants collecting
in the space just past my doormat by 2:45am they are
gone I will never know what they have carried away
or if they were ever really there to begin with

Dear Lettera 32,
I send a message to you I am surprised you see it I'm
surprised that you're right there. you say nothing hope
I can feel you smiling I am yet I envy this. your
ability to say nothing

Dear Lettera 32,

the flying ants are back I didn't see them arrive I
pull back the curtains open the window for the ants I
am perpetually opening windows in my night these
sequences, letters with and on your machine they're
still. all yours

Dear Lettera 32,

"what's the worst that could happen" remains my least
loved question. I cannot leave this room full of all my
answers. risk is an embodiment of precarity. I see a
doctor because I have run out of options. I write
better when no one is listening the serial force of the
utterance appearing on paper the poem. punched in to
want my body. is to want. at least desire something to
love me back

Dear Lettera 32,
I must ask to become. a medical subject after I said I.
would do this no more perhaps being at risk is to always
be begging for my life one way or another I stay. awake
for another 24 hours without sleep my mouth is full. of
frangipanis.blossoms blossoms blossoms I think I can
see something burning in the.distance something like a
fire flickering on the underside of thick clouds gathered
I return to the window. a moment later and the light is
gone.I wonder if it was ever really there on page 60 of
My Life Lyn Hejinian says "As for we who love to be
astonished, the night is lit."

Dear Lettera 32,
the worst part of this irony is staged in places of
risk and fate I feel. my way through. my fears first
then yours as though my fate might be your fault body.
bound up in the affect of our combined dreamings this:
inarticulate connection of precarity and worry a way
through all these. hours of waking waiting to be sent
read responded to.

Dear Lettera 32,

I am trying to believe. in destiny in my body as
containing. energy more than exhaustion there isn't a
single pharmacy on the island that supplies the
medication I need I have to go. to the hospital an
attempt at access the ironic. juxtaposition of risk by
medication is nothing. short of astounding.don't talk
to me about supply chains and capitalist violence an
incoming I don't remember. the last place for the poem
to come from the acoustic analogue of the typewriter
this percussive record each words pushed out against.
the page each ink tap ting a memory ongoing perhaps
this my alphabet has become a recollection of force
my necessary travel is to SGH Singapore General Hospital
when I am leaving I pass an old man diasporic Chinese
Singaporean leaning on the arm of his wife in a t-shirt
that read "HUGS NOT DRUGS" I keep my head down.
collected my own chemical self care after 4 months
missing care. taker is equivalent to drug. taker each
opioid each hug an ingesting of the same kindness

Dear Lettera 32,

I don't want. to be in this, much pain anymore this.
reality of constraint an audience. of no one for this
to work one of us has to be hopeless or at least romantic
I don't believe. this I don't. know why. I am here. I
can only hope. hope that you do too

Dear Lettera 32
                / part 2

Dear Lettera 32,

what will I hear, when you go. this afternoon is my turn
in sadness. and half-formed hearings I couldn't tell. a
whether Connan Mockasin sings lovely lucky or lonely a
voice effervescent. sad and sexy hope I have felt you. an
excursive collection of flight and arrivals I don't know.
how to take back or hope my way out. your inconsolable arms.
around me falling into another out of placeness our last
spoken utterances are "take care" "you too" there's a
part of me that knows I'll never be together in spirit
"let's try and be American just for the hell of it"
Ariana Reines June 4th I wake up at 4am wondering what I'm
supposed to do. with my teeth

Dear Lettera 32,

amid the tiles and pictures of us is you in minutes in
wanting the next part of this softness meaninglessness
legs still shaking all this waiting into the unknown
writing what I disbelieve I believe the paper is involuting
directly against the visible a student says "your
cosiness vibes are off the chart" and I know I am
recuperating you're teaching over Zoom with a virtual
background a publisher poet the black and white picture
you've put elephants in the room visually unequivocally
their outlines and skeletons witty and audacious I put
the cover of the anthology I'm co-publishing behind me
hope you can see the stitches I yield you all still love
in metaphor wine out of open glass jam jars of memory.
its insistent lucidity I fold into your arms and a
huddle occurs you become a circle inside numbers of time
running out "what we're doing as writers is trying to
write it" typewriting a curling back of spooling language
seeking solitude and someplace to come back to

Dear Lettera 32,

every part of this may be unspeakable I've spent all year
in poetry. and in person promising not to. get you into
trouble you. mispronounce intimate (the verb) as intimate
(the adjective) and suddenly every fate takes shape as
a Freudian slip typewriting itself is. a search for
force "I thought someone was swinging a battle axe in my
kitchen I'll carry that with me that was remarkable" to
our most profound texts genre doesn't really apply we
don't. sleep and keep all our rings on my eyes. are too
drawn to your name the sunset a student writes a poem
that ends I hope somebody dies. tomorrow the last line's
a killer and the poet might still get their wish the
classroom deciding a space for which. one of us dies hope
our annihilation to stay. up all night staring at the
thunderstorm mutual in its magic. entirely a moment to
carry with you to the end of every last line

Dear Lettera 32

I begged you to stop hurting me then I begged you not
to stop they bleach all the stairs outside you said
falling down them twice "I think all my work is pretty
pathetic" Eileen Myles November 11th typing this
transmission perpetually leaving impressions in this
island too the panopticonic place I want to know what it
would mean to move in the world completely defenceless
to concede desire's slightest fragment my overlapping
all this way past "all my poems are pathetic" Eileen
Myles November 11th I've been running towards lighthearted
like it's all one word the image of the gloaming your
brother sent you high driving miles to see I know you
are happier with sunlight in your eyes I miss your hands
in the space where mine have been perhaps I'm just as
delirious

Dear Lettera 32,
best of luck. with everything I send hope you'll be home.
soon I know what it means when you remove the bones you.
put on your chest I cut my teeth on the softest edges of
your voice "that's the face I was hoping for" I am still.
lying on the floor in the dark staring upwards hope you've
been. in my work for months didn't notice until. how
everyone else did and no one is. surprised why don't I
believe. in destiny I dream a thunder of your fingers five
days before your hands were in my hair and I was close.
to kissing you "what if people spy on you in your dreams
by dreaming themselves into them?" Alice Notley November
25th at three in the morning I wake up knowing. something
about you had changed when I sat up somewhere else in that
night you curled your body about mine and everything in
me turned tenderness your leaving wasn't quiet it was so
full. of music hope and the poem. writes a motivation out.
of one problem and into another I didn't know. I needed.
just between you and me there's always been a real world
I'm trying not to love you there

Dear Lettera 32,
hope you're so fucking soft you teach your last. two
classes over Zoom interrupted by a student who says you're
too quiet in all the right places. you ask that too. i
said to your students you're laughing and we're knowing
why I will profess. to being defenceless confess to that
much Singapore an inescapable Catholicism it's been. three
days and i'm still looking. out for your eyes in their
infinite blueness

Dear Lettera 32,
how are you? I still feel amphoteric

Dear Lettera 32,
we lay on the floor watching shadows left by the rain
just to see if we were right fuck why did i have to
fall for love in you listen to you sleeping believing
everything you said when you were inside me i think i
will never be in love with even the barest modicum of
grace there are other things to do in a lifetime when
i do this it's often about my own accountability" Ariana
Reines November 13th these are still all yours operating
around sleep or hiding or another place of wanting to hear
your voice again

Dear Lettera 32,

hope is a force and a resource. anhedonic anagogical the
necessary sense of futility I am struggling to get back.
to everyone ghost. enchantment is an energy I won't succumb.
to and this is my refusal to hide I am still trying. to
measure the distance of suddenly I have no density. you
could pass. hope all the way through me. English is a
second hypoglossia. you said shelter in the still partial
apparitional spectra recuperating a direction. towards
refuge rather than rupture the analogy doesn't work. both
ways you said when I tell. you about running. away in
this allusion hope am I failing. my own marshmallow test
as though re-membering Eeyore makes his sadness complete
in his melancholy he can experience it still. not
looking for what's fallen off him or has been taken. away
in a mind of separation I am scattered and abandonment
keeps. on happening a deranging affect pile on of extremity
in Singapore. to taupok refers to a pack of males
flinging. themselves one on top the other one lying
prostrate. on the ground you make third-rate men of all
my lyric. i's I don't know for how long I will stay.
hereditary maybe someday the embodiment of my being will
be measured. in metric distance I am still. running away
from my gut

Dear Lettera 32,
I want, to be held in inerrancy what is a poet exhausted.
not sleeping homesick dissolving without thinking. I
look up and reply "lyrically ashamed" I hang. your drafts
up in my room cover the walls in the first instances of
your hands comfortably fill the space between them. your
hugs are still better "kinship and solidarity and that is
why I write" Jordan Scott October 21st poetry as intimate,
community a safety that keeps, ongoing I know. I'm looking
for something or maybe just the rest of it

Dear Lettera 32,

maybe we're both wild funky man girls thunderstruck for
thought on the floor. together watching for the
indistinguishable. feeling lucky lovely lonely hope I'm
scared. I will never stop thinking about you neither of us
knowing. what is about to happen come. back I'm sorry
what're you apologising for the back of my hand. brushed
against you you. can brush me with the back of your hand
anytime you like well. shit I can see another country.
out my window I steal. my name from the front of the door.
before I leave this poem is time. only it will tell how.
"voices. weave intimacy. transcendence" Danielle Vogel.
November 22nd I still want to run. away with you a scale
we're both sharing still listening out for. I don't know
how else to write without. typing a commitment to what we
both know. to be true the infinite distance. of desire and
fidelity my undoing

Dear Lettera 32,

I am accumulating. text a force through which to get to
an elsewhere in this year. human connection a flex fear
in breath.colour this present. an uncanny writing as
though I don't know I'll never get away. with it I can see
the monsoon. spell gathering from my window on the "Longing,
thirteenth floor the distance slowly disappearing.
we say. because desire is full of endless distances.
Robert Hass. how many times can I say hope. I never want
to see you again for you to know I mean the exact
opposite you are so far away. distance is so full of
desire. and full is so distant. so land this way.
longing is full of distances so desire. endlessly

Dear Lettera 32,

we're both scared aren't we hope. hiding closest to my
spine the nape of my neck at your back's smallest place.
across thousands of miles is the same beauty of the moon
I can't shrug it off either I know I'm asleep when I've
stopped. listening looking up. at the instant. sky without
our names on it pretending there's a place to reach our
bloodlines without moving through it the common. sense
of the shared we commune. as we communicate a way out. of
this season the poem an inverse operation. how far are we.
bound by the next. slide if we can go there. imagining
after the end of it hope I tell you I am small. and of
little consequence and you reply with emoji-ed scepticism
"write a spell. I will know if it's working" Robert.
Majzels.September 16th to write this out is to cast it.
in ink in each spelling of your name on page 62 of The
Language of Inquiry Lyn Hejinian writes "can one take
captives by writing. the "one" (first) is "I." hope did
I put a poem on you! do you know. how much this will
accumulate

Dear Lettera 32,
could magic and the poem be cast in subdermal frequencies
I find myself catching your hands my notes the typewriter
it is easier to write when I believe no one is paying me to
be exhausted is to contain a venom of minor feeling hope
your sound is the imminent last line of the Ashbery poem
you keep taped to your door but night the reserved the
reticent gives more than it takes " in 1978 Miyoko Ito
said "I have no place to take myself except painting" this
year has been so full of surprises prophet hero
distractingly gendered all hail "I don't know if what goes
on inside me deserves to be called thinking" Gunnar
Wærness November 20th you told me to say thank you so I
do I have no place to take myself except poetry hope are
you lonely lovely lucky I'm still writing around it what
we both know to be true

Dear Lettera 32,
lying on the floor you're talking. about the thong genre
of music and all I can think is god. hope. if my econonium
should sound so good. someday a casting this crafting a
glimpse. of the negative light this desire to tell. remove
blood with makeup wipes and it will stay. red for twice
as long. this lyric eccymosis all night. re-fugue-ing is
delirious still I want to be thunder and enlightening

Dear Lettera 32,

am I allowed to tell you everything. put the bones back
by your name red panther paw bird beak I haven't slept.
with anyone.I wasn't in love with. in years.no one should
take me seriously.defenceless. and saying thank you "maybe
I don't understand all the languages that address my body"
Erin Moure.November 20th.this indented.recording of what
I'm like when I'm alone "Not that I think it would surprise
you. Everyday.I see the unbearable beauty and sanity of
your eyes, which.know everything about me." Franz Wright
listening.about it. now and you hope. a stretching of
re-fused.fibres pushing tape against the carriage audibly
sensemaking.all true and reeling. away from me. I see shapes
I want to dissolve. my thinking this I am. eclipse hope
and retrograde imbricating how do we "destroy" you you ask
your students you say "it's different every time"

Dear Lettera 32,

hope are you still scrolling. for euphoria or the sound
of it. you say that. I'm allowed to ask you anything at
any time forever what should I do with this. in gathering
hope without return Singapore still has more money than
sense "I like the coat hangers" "they're weird" "weird is
good" "weird is all we've got" the imprint of our heads.
still in the pillows set out on the floor that's cute
you said chaos is still a type of knowledge I ask my
supervisor to use my pronouns in a form. nobody reads he
says he. doesn't want to include anything distracting.
that's the reference I don't care if I land. him in.
trouble he has enough money to get out without needing to
write. a poem the irresistible urge to profess. something
I am called "half-British" by a prize-winning author
complicity is searching. through 23 years to cite it's
location he doesn't tell. me anything. else only it's there
and he knows. it naming me my halfness whitening. hope
bending away what are we. contingent in passing when the
truth demands to be wet it's just sea infringement it all
still is

Dear Lettera 32,

I'm still writing out my invocation to poetry as craft
and spell as an alignment of energy in this scrolling I
don't know how to name what comes with me across this
machine a lyric foam you must've said that somewhere before
me I walk past the clinic and forget the word for bleach.
the paper wound. all the way up I think I can smell the
sanity

Dear Lettera 32,

the last occupant of this room was monolidded adhering
tape crosses every surface had this comforted her this
special light I never meant to put it down it's all still.
here the quiet mechanism the black desk I am less
frightened by permanence or the constancy of the mistake
every sound we make is a bit of autobiography" Anne
Carson in this acoustic apperception I can't believe this
is happening the shit I used to read about "Please let
me know if this reached you. I will not intrude on your
life in any way. But I miss you so much." Franz Wright as
though it had never been folded back in the first place
the poem a punctuation punch future suture sutra lovely
lucky lonely homesickness is still a type of sickness at
4pm each winter day it rains another machinic recording

Dear Lettera 32,

"in writing my gender becomes genre" Mary Reufle am I
writing a non-binary genre to you to centre me in this.
imprint against erasure. a duende.danger so far deathless
oblivion to speak. so close is this an act of edging.
along the margins taking pleasure. in refusing the fine.
at the level of sentencing the typewriter. has no key for
the number one every time I need one I must type. 1 what
does 1 do. in keying all this in hope. is a force against
the carriage the poem. another transportation coiling
radially in whorls largely invisible to see. the scroll
extend unrolling from this site. is to become coherent. in
what is sent hope. the vibratory absorbing. in rows of
matter the paper pressed against itself slowing. down the
rate of perception I can touch. every part of the process
inches of paper being impressed by the extent of objection
uncurling. the legible at night and just before dawn
becoming visible again

Dear Lettera 32,

light still collects. at a distance perhaps the ivory.
tower has more than one window or wavelength for looking
out the coloured light of a dimension not yet arrived
Mei-Mei Berssenbrugge the machine is a construct and a
constraint hope. are you intractable in all these. rows a
strange invitation to circular time keep. going in constant
hypotaxis arching. back the paper flattening under itself
mishearing alters the dimensions of the word turning. with
each click ancillary bodies that move. away from each.
other through language. in its littleness hope are you a
total imagining a defencelessness comfort consequence the
tease or something entirely outside writing

Dear Lettera 32,
is this contradiction another hope. for proximity

Dear Lettera 32,
I cannot hold onto visibility or language all doomscrolling.
backwards the poem the hundred sing. dollar moment hope
in proportion. to this cylinder the object of focus in the
distance the dark is radiant and unfathomable there are
so many. emanations wineglasswineglasspancakespizzablake
oppenspotifyicedcoffeehypotheticalvodkashotthetypewriter
I don't contain a frequency of innocence. when light turns
out speech even colour is still a vibration is hope a
paratext a thousand different feet all walking. the
outwards shattering. in which the first form is always
futile." when looking at the fragment we're still talking
about the disaster" maybe to be eccentric is to be left
to your own devices hope I have left all myself to yours

Dear Lettera 32,
maybe cliché is caring about something more than the dog
does about his day. chthonic rather than cathartic my parents
send photos of the sunrise bright and breaking hope.
there are days I will never wake up to close to another
time and another way of feeling

Dear Lettera 32,

please see me. through this metonymy I have. moments of
paranoia in which I believe every plant around me has
been replaced with a plastic duplicate take it like
dreaming. the poem of your hands. the speech impediment
of thunder. I don't know what I'm about to say I neverknow
what I'm about to say read me. out I dare. you in the
mouth you keep. hope you will always be indelible

Dear Lettera 32,

I do not sleep a wink and remember all my dreams a
company in all these rows rows rows the object in
this address I'm still a coward even when I'm alone in
pain perhaps I've always been closer to delirium living on
the outskirts of town I like the art of poetry precisely
Ariana Reines December 7th is this all another hurtling
endlessly summoned into being nowhere near me what will
you say about me here in this metabolic primacy I don't
want to be the last one left agglutinating being even
now with the texture of your fingertips hope get to the
end of the page I know I'll meet you there

Dear Lettera 32,

do I want to run out of longing for you or do I just
want to spend all day here the mercy hour in real mouths
all these weeks. I know I shouldn't be counting the days
every distance across the page. write me a poem I will
know if it is working

Dear Lettera 32,

perhaps chronic is another preoccupation. with chthonic
your leaving is so fast. what is the poem bent on
becoming underneath itself out. from me one mouth late.
you said you spent your twenties breaking up with everyone
all this could be. unspeakable is delirium. another
fragment this time of sense. my capacity for exhaustion
in the poem. I love everyone the way I want to hope I'll
be. with you without reuniting the need to know this
lonely lucky lovely way in. the world

Dear Lettera 32,
to stay in work stay in love, but hope there are still
moments for joy coming in days for both of us. I
receive a parcel in the post inside is an Olivetti Lettera
32 and fifteen metres of light

Dear Lettera 32 / part 3

Dear Lettera 32,

I sign off every letter yours endlessly, hope before
the moment I know, what you've already done there's an
art to leaving well and you've, done everything wrong
fuck any word you ever felt for me. but rage is one,
dimensional and just. as resistant hope a disintegration
of everything you've said about me all, over again I
know I'm the victim of something left here, tracing out
what you've done that l. was right after the fact

Dear Lettera 32,

I am trying to remember. everyone is out of their minds
in one. way or another i am a poet. I a large pile of
nonsense." I hate that you don't feel shocked by feeling
sad." E.P. Jenkins December 23rd requesting convergence
to believe the twilight zone of a face "talking about
the sublime doesn't make it sublime" Khaled Hakim
December 23rd I am here to take my body. back hope
failure and innocence the typewriter the ultimate
reelness.a device the paper circulating itself out. the
winding in inarticulate extemporisation welcome to the
commonwealth of third-rate men in all of my i's in your
silence. the body you didn't the body you did both. left
behind in the unaccountable. distance and all that time
you'll never be able to come. back in finitude lies.
the certainty of the dawn hope. and no more quivering

Dear Lettera 32,

there's hope you try to take and fail I. am gifted a
ring older than both of us in silver. a circle I keep
and drink this festival to your abstraction how do I do
this and give everything. away alone with the hope you
did. wrong out of the blue in your eyes when she asks
"were all the nice things you said about my work just
foreplay" I hope you never recover my body. a measure of
white cis male decency you. are all of those why did I
ever hope you were innocent even just. for a second the
way I look at you won't. do it again. all outrage and
limerence E.P. Jenkins asks "what could you do to hold
him accountable" I said I. can write a poem

Dear Lettera 32,
how are you? I hope you never teach again

Dear Lettera 32,
I believed you when you said poetry was the place you
take your body. to be renewed on the tip of your tongue
where mine disappears did you. find the place you were
looking for in my quiet. face you get back. into trouble
it's not my nightmares this time hope I cannot stay in
any kind of unconsciousness. when I say fuck your mom
I'm referring to the men that raised you every institution
that pays. you poet by professor profession Singapore
is still 100% possession and you overwhelmed. all of me
we're holding. hands here the bodies you tried on the
one you swept away I keep. wondering what they'll think
of. you the poets and people you. love if they knew.
what you were. like in this false corner of the world I
am. still alone trying to take this device back in. the
depths of this unwinding to see your eyes again and
hope nothing

Dear Lettera 32,

they're on another plane you said when you were talking
about mt being in pain alters. my way of hoping. here i
know i am. hurt hearing from those who still think well
of you and see beauty as a pursuit where the poem
ought to be hope. in flight with the winterside of your
voice i'm watching back the video of you naming. animals
on the edge of extinction i'm delirious you said and i
haven't stopped. thinking a bout of it acutely none of
it will. save you it will not save you the record. turns
through all the music and on. into another langue again
you. know this take me into silence and suffer to hope.
here is to be entirely. self-referential if you ever
cared tell me why. either of us a script of all undoing
i will never trust it. again the sun in both your eyes

Dear Lettera 32,

do you like running away searching for a general. theory
of escape or something against capture in me. in hope I
have learnt so much. from you this year Alphonso Lingis
David Foster Wallace Dean. Young the organisation. of
style how to use a body at a distance. a cockerel cries.
outside my window each morning accompanying the dawn
hiding. your name as it gets fight again Theodore Hopf
is fired from NUS the National University of Singapore
on December 1st

Dear Lettera 32,

as the record returns I hope you the world's lowest
immunity to poetry. in this grace fall of your tongue
where mine has been so full. of surprises I hope you.
hear this in absentia after. hope your body in. all that
White American Guilt "when I talk about your mom she's
actually standing in for wider socio-political categories"
you said. when I talk about mom I'm talking about your
manpower the ministry of it

Dear Lettera 32,

perhaps I'm not, as safe here as I thought, I was to
reel into equanimity the keys in their eternal
flickering I swear my heart off, the poets wouldn't do
it, again either to make sense, of all those snow lines
twice over hope, like love and writing is an ongoing,
project no two keys can strike the same time, if two are
pressed together both stop neither making, it to the
surface perhaps it was never safe, to desire legibly at
all I should have believed, you in my dreams when you
told me not to when you strangled me to death in my
nightmares in May the way you traced, your fingers across
my shoulders after reading Jordan Scott I know I am
quiet might, never manage to hate or achieve rage
without dexterity or unpliable sadness I remember how
close, you stood to homesick will I finally cast it here
the word I've been, swerving into the propelled metal to
print, it out just once, typesetting against the surface
to utter lust

Dear Lettera 32,

to write is as much an act as to do "you're allowed to ask
me anything at any time forever I'm an open book" you
said when did you think to write as much an act as
your student and I the typewriter, is heavy enough to
carry, this calling outwards the poem the roll call I
know you'll never face up to it "encomium – an ancient
term for a flattering speech – is an anagram of meconium –
the shit we are full of at birth" Anne Boyer December 21st
perhaps to be pathetic here is to hope, uselessly
recalcitrant and restless the typewriter the brute
confrontation, with loss the paper still passing, in sheets
you still live, in style a lurid organisation of truth
unspeakably gone to hope, and never look back as I walk.
home my world returns ultraviolet the typewriter a
history of my absorption the machine archive of your
eyes every last purr in your throat in the energy of the
moment you know which one you are still, staring at the
hooks the ones you'll never get out I know you're still
licking them clean

Dear Lettera 32,

in dreams remember your own escape hope when I am
scared I instinctively ask your advice your childhood
of loss the pressure to excel familial rivalry a lack
of unconditional love an enormous sense of entitlement
in each instance you reached out to touch I hope it
unsettles you the Persian rug the poem I gave you 2
days before you took off all my clothes and dropped 16
hours behind me faith can throw everything up this frame
and endless accrual your own attempts at filling that
hole where God once taught you I know you're still
responsible I'm fleeing from place to poetry and back to
place again

Dear Lettera 32,
I avoid all myself socially atomising it's Christmas
Day and I don't sleep see through every opening in
another 24 hours I spend my first night away from the
typewriter I can't tell daytime by the colour of the
sky the way I can at night driving through sunset rain
this writing is an emphatic listening listing the truth
is sometimes ineffable perhaps the belief was always
more beautiful and that is a way to go on in infinite
attention to hope

Dear Lettera 32,

you're ruled by Saturn you use the same lines twice to
speak. under whatever star planet sky body happens. to
be in retrograde I. still don't know how you pass. the
end of the poem to follow in love. the most violent act
with unbreakable silence I should have seen this. coming
imminence on a vibrational level perhaps I. did and
failed to translate the energetic freqnence a resonancy
into language this perspicacious absence. in time I tell.
you I'm not inclined towards jealousy "that's for people
who don't know what they've got" you said sleeplessly
I see the secretly terrible parts of you I know you
will never speak to me again"

Dear Lettera 32,

I'm at capacity with myself hope, for reel this time
this, relation an infestation dissolved and released a
structural anxiety days after, the fact the sun is shining
it, rains over a double rainbow "if you know you like
something you are a target" when you said it in August
were you looking at the whiteboard..hope somewhere else
in the room i'm still looking, for its inflections "that's
what people with stable jobs do is try not to be a
menace to society" Ariana Reines December 20th in
gathering concurrently the present speaks the future the
poem, putting it together this contact the ants the bug
and getting bitten I am visited by a gecko it sits by
my light and shows me its toes I can't remember, the
word for wanting, to be burnt rather than buried, to know
who. I have slept with the con-sumer the material work
the contagion of oblivion, I'll leave, it over the border
of poesies and the lunar boundary, of writing at night
what will this do, to you hope the transformational
parts the machine evolving we're, never done with
upheaval still working, out the catastrophes I go, back
in time and remember mishearing you you cover your face
with your hands and say I'm deleterious

Dear Lettera 32,
when you talk about Alphonso Lingis you say "it's fine
if he needs to get between my legs to give a good reading
that's fine like whatever" whe literally opened that
sarcophagus between my legs" does it feel like a
dispensation from on high inescapable Americanness
psychological conflict and ironic distance hope and
poetry won't make you a kind person won't protect you.
from anything weaponised injurious ruinous precise
connivances I want to get back to the mechanism I'm in.
too much pain to move I know I'm frightening the death.
my body is always suggesting that time you want to be
held in

Dear Lettera 32,

I might as well give you the line's share there are no
commons I find. the beginnings of water tell the present.
it knows what's to come "there's a difference between
feeling lucky and being fortunate" you say with the
fortuned. texture of your voice hope. tear it down wake
up and save one this. haunted now turning. down or backwards
ever present or primeval turpitude will always carry.
the sound. of your voice I must have freaked. you out
that morning when I said it sounded so good on you the
dash the tender. cessation a softness rotting the hyphen
the lick split scheme I know you're still living to get
away. with it

Dear Lettera 32,

the letters still dent the paper ghost undersides and ink
less markings the typewriter keys all beating this
repercussion I have always hoped with violet intensity
this is no different in the poem you are multiple and
so am I the future pressing into the present "these
kids" you said half laughing shaking disbelief off your
head are they kids to you I ask excluding my body from
the category you tell me a story about age and sight
without mirrors describing youth as something you keep
under your skin it doesn't answer the question I am so
shit at being woman there are many kinds of transmission
you overdose on surrender the moment you read everything
still sapphirine the stars recite it all and are even more
ashamed

Dear Lettera 32,

we know what you're guilty. of take your time attention
solidity an account.i can't believe. he's writing his
memoirs he has nothing else. left to write poetry to
survive. you the only place i could go to space out. this
perfidy this distortion the typewriter the gorgeous
warfare you said you needed rage. has imparted me.
recompense i am all the way open.i know. your tattoos
reading the recording flesh. wounds all the ones you
touched.we know your eyes in every second. imagination
metabolising the dawn and all the ways my mind might.
change for an hour. for another.i. don't percieve this
connection. to survive time is innumerable each line.
break happening in air space up from inside the technology
my fingers are. footprints utterly ambivalent. to cohere
or condemn nothing. about this poetry will make you a
good person not by any stretch that spell which sits over.
language the weapon that haunts. is every single way the
mantra goes in to pay for it without getting. a grip i
won't enter this. economy to be in my body i weep. to
make my person mine promise you. hope will not austere me
i know this is. a long way to try and explain the decked.
out stars to spell out renewal sentence.you to saturninity
and hope. an unintelligible safety we will never move on
will. never move on never. move on

Dear Lettera 32,

in this much pain to have. a body is not a safe wanting.
bound up in trust and in. loving to hope is to hold
every capacity "there are poets I think I'd still be
friends with if I hadn't been so insecure" you said once
it was dark culpability and the past both tensions
ghosting the light in its coldness there are many things
I kept once. the music stopped and you turned off the
lights clandestine silence my body all the way in love
sonancy and wholeness I am spacing you out of place on
this typewriter under the moon with the precise enormity
of hope and houses of light after taking everything we
hold. every possibility still. with your disgrace

Dear Lettera 32,

in hope a new order I reset the margins clearing lever
bail rods I rewind the ribbon for the third time the
poem the place for it in obscurity it's necessary
flippancy to hope without reconcile the white American
appetite for cruelty when no one else is looking half red.
tape in this the softest recourse to enmity on page 68
of My Life Lyn Hejinian says "The screen can be taken
away from the fire as long as someone is sitting in the
room" hopelessly the ultimate contranym you astonish voice.
from my mouth the moment you ask if I want to hear you
beg I thought I was I try everything I waited all this
took a year me you we her I the typewriters of poetry its
repeated framings I'm not asking permission anymore
writing someplace elsewhere

Dear Lettera 32,

I am still in love without the informal second-person
singular pronoun the non-arrival gap before the eyelet
guided centre there is a difference between exhaustion
and the empty spool keep it see what happens this is
all there is to you the bygone machine another
consoling hour

Dear Lettera 32,

let's pretend I still love you.let's pretend that I can't
in sheets closest to. my body imploding I am all inward
I will see it. through to the end the spell speaking
the poem season decoction this missive a public.
dreaming to revoke the surge of your jaws. at my neck
when you took my throat. between your teeth I'll retract
all your blood. and pathos but I haven't forgiven.
you hope every definition of grace I type. faster
than I used to in this liquid. lyric and hope gives
every last word

Dear Lettera 32,

I couldn't write you, till now a lyric contraction
lunation and vanishing i. couldn't get round the back
of it I have come to the unreel. the letter the love the
elegy you. will keep on turning the poem place where
words will be, recalled and look. like light to fight
back violence's aim for beauty

Dear Lettera 32,
when I walk towards the gloaming the moon is. at my
shoulders saying you. is just me. talking to myself again
in this lysosomal lyric pressed between here and
newly born the half.light has taken. my head to hope in
wonder.and delectation there. it is you. the real you
of poetry. which can only go on hope I go on. hope go
on go on go on

Dear Lettera 32 / part 4

Dear Lettera 32,
the poem is, real and everything falters the black crow,
black hens four small chicks in the bougainvillea plants
outside Cantonment Police Complex. I see thunder and
hear nothing on enigma look at the fumes responsibility
and love are inextricable and limitless. I believe you
and hope it's still here the almanac predicts this too
attending to it endlessly

Dear Lettera 32,

is this the jaw of an outlaw hope, against legibility,
legitimacy innocence and respectability desire against
pragmatism pleasure. in typing out the tactile world the
paper is bailing itself out imprinting an awareness. to
dreams re-enchanting the imagination. reality gets
jostled and something is opened in that process. Jackie
Wang I avow and make present measuring the joints of
female fate I ask E. P. Jenkins if to loom is also to be.
impending about the relation of addiction to instinct
hope I'm so sorry. about his eyes the way they kept me.
breathing

Dear Lettera 32,
in this, country of elemental summertime Jurong Island
is designed for toxic chemical manufacturing this body
bequeathed by the ocean hope is a measure. Of my decency
or anybody else's this has all happened since I know. I
love in consternation to recall you somatically into me
soma the mechanisation contraption, conception I hope
like the rain I know I will be. questioned to death how
do you sicken the chronically ill the infinitely sick I
want to learn to fuck without fear without fair without
fur without fearing again perhaps to be on another,
frequency is to be akin to feral or in some way derived
from ferocious

Dear Lettera 32,
am I menacing?

Dear Lettera 32,
I would be honest about everything. ideally hope and
tumescence. I built this for you a sunrise garrulous
frowzy ensorcellating today. love makes everything
levitate I live off Jalan Bahar this autocorrects jalan
baha in Bahasa Indonesia this is the path of the language
empty spaces of tonal denotation empty spaces of total
detonation I'm waiting to see how American you get. in
this ever expansive whitening this is still not over in
the daybreak dimension colour is pure and flying

Dear Lettera 32,
hope how do I confess when pain has taken up every
language available I'm trying to do this without
premeditation premedication preamble or prediction. the
queer crip poet survivals are still the ones I look up to.
I cannot speak. in the biometrics of my body dreaming. and
redemption I am perpetually under. my own skin hope I know
what I take small and white and wonder. as its dailyness
dissipates into my blood does it know me as well as it
knows us all. sense and insensible giving a shit. about
gender means I want to shit all over it "language is what
makes the wounds come open again" Anne Carson infirming
this state of uninterrupted disaster what does it amount
to. a sonic congealing crip precession pain like hope is
scatological dysfluent dyssomniatic dysphoric dysmorphic
to hope. in the poem see all my audacities. shifting in
half-sense the register reaching all our days I lose the
surface of my tongue watching myself dissolve time. has
no wings but subsists. in our bones a crisis of metric
bombardment and hope a kind of radiation

Dear Lettera 32,
"to be on the edge means sitting with that loneliness"
Marylyn Tan January 27th to be sudden is to be without
lingering or fair. warning even blood is still a stream.
open the world as you know it true art must rid sanity of
prejudice. I misread it and medicine contains the promise
of care hope I am love hungry my heart a black jelly a
baby soft head between teeth disembowelled disembodied
disembarked I still avoid my lecturers when I know I'm not
okay "what's up with you, you're as white as a sheet"
exhaustion is an aesthetic statement euphoric and
distending in time altering the resonance of my body the
thudding inhospitality of my gut "My kids have got the
sniffles and have been told not to come to school for a
week - are you well enough to be here?" "Do you need to
go see a doctor?" replaying the moment of the approach in
sudden cotton sheet whiteness is it that, obvious I ask
half as much myself. as hope writing in pain I know. I
will never get out of it hypnotically rapturous it moves
with totalising speed and with every precision of truth

Dear Lettera 32,

I am muzzled and ejected from the nest domesticity of the
ablebodied background "the problem of the poet is the
problem of the life in nerves" Peter Gizzi February 3rd
I am learning to live without line breaks hope in full
sentences. get to the end of the page we took.
fortification from goneness a minor enunciation, of margins
a survival that is tight-fitting where is the female
polarity of my tongue its idle chance my body betrothed
to the scale veiling the illusion of the last impatient
percentage femmefolk you and so this accrues line by
excruciating line

Dear Lettera 32,
I move the turquoise frame back into its box, again hope
is restless a long sun trying to reconcile the machine
with myself hope folds, back sound from the place voice
takes away to find, you is to type out your full name in
force, across the keys I am irreverent and irrelevant all
blood and pressure in the absence of reliable ghosts I
made an aria Meena Alexander hope the passing, sensation
of hazard as fear looks more like the rain I think I've
slept I'm not sure, anymore I know my suffering doesn't
make me, special hope illuminates my geometric negations
and makes us unimaginable

Dear Lettera 32,
hope and the poem are a minor reparative magic. I have.
no desire to resemble. testimony by any other names
hectic red I type to view a wireless ghost she looks at
me with eyes that have finally replaced your own and asks
"have I been listening to a lunatic?" we laugh knowing
with the same brown light that the answer is yes. I will
not close. my heart. my work will not live like an
overdose paranoia or eunoia hope beyond the rational
capacity carnivalesque and dewy pain has a big meaning.
it is nothing that we're here at all it is not my body
which included the world "if I suffered what else would
I do" Bernadette Mayer February 20th but write incomplete
thoughts into poetry

Dear Lettera 32,

the night after my first tattoo I dream I am a hound I
run on all fours grab his body. by my open mouth and rip
off his head he fears this child as a highway separated
from his neck he is a single tooth and I am elated I
watch the jungle out my window the day before the hearing
the sunset is so close. to red moments later the gloaming
is gone fine clouds and high. rise the social houses are
skyscrapers I disassociate from the back of my throat.
the declaration taking place. in broad daylight I'm not
trying to be charming. Poetry proves me. I don't give a
shit what happens now Eileen Myles hope should I be found
in factuality. the shortest moment before the committee
and all their rhetorical speech I know this. has never
worked. pain makes useless things of memory my heart is
drunk on untestable agony I am responsible only to death

Dear Lettera 32,
Rikei gifts me a red fire Pokemon card and asks will you
evolve hope. I want the body a coward would be ashamed of
how does survivor identity function when the encounter is
never. ending the brevity. of rainfall this virtue fluency
I dream of being. shot while doing the shooting "Will you?
Will you?" Alice Notley March 8th be. still substitute If
pain for trauma here. or acute sickness your choice If
you're both at the same conference he's the one that should
be running Winnie Sung March 11th I know I'm not.
leaving I think I'm safer. here hope ratiocination I know
who to be. frightened by. in pain all the exaggerations
are true for ow is so close to awe and the beeping of our
hearts in this hideout nothing. can be done but to keep.
saying it

Dear Lettera 32,

there's a phonetic translation and a typo in my full name
maybe someday I'll tell you the moon is ridiculous.
caught in this hazardous medium of light "Hi I just wanted
to tell you you're beautiful" says a stranger by the train
"You're not fully Chinese are you?" "Looking at you makes
me happy" I'm waiting for the utterance to seem less
strange to become a practical joke or another encounter
entirely you have the most beautiful eyes I know I'm
afraid of the gaze I wanted to believe you didn't have a
bad hope in your body "Joe Brainard must've been the
cutest guy you've ever seen for how often he gets
propositioned" you said before your heart turned ugly and
unflinching the light is no escape "Just say thank you"
you said like an incisor running towards the crossroads
outside in the sun just to keep moving away on March 20th
I make peace with the walls the red ink fading into the
record of the local and inaudible I'm not sure what kind
of hoping this is anymore not sure I ever was

Dear Lettera 32,

"to write of death is to write of everyone" Anne Boyer I
want an unknown destruction a synonym for antagonist. is
crip a synonym for crip is bad I bear the intensity. of
this distress all hope attuned to these concerns. you
deserve the peace of living and life Sonia Sanchez March
26th I still get painkillers from SGH it's been almost a
year now at the dispensary. a man remembers this he sees
me and says "I'm disappointed" you might want to get used
to seeing me or I'll disappoint you more often is it a
dependency" he asks a chronically sick sort of "if it's
over prescribed we won't be able to dispense it to you
anymore remember the government is watching" March 30th I
go home in a profound cremation of silence as love falls
in the sky hope is a colour outside the birth of radiance
calamansi on cut lips

Dear Lettera 32,
what makes your eyes roll in your heart. every time you hear
it. hope. is a cultural medium the locus where it sits
dying and failure give the same sense of permission. he
died he can say anything. Barrie Sherwood April 7th witness
to vulnerability with every mark comes. out. sound the
typewriter a series of embeddings kindness has. scarred me
like a supine grove hope an intimate wilderness. we want
to know if what we hope is enough we'll never know. if it
is it is. possible to hurt without harm history is legacy's
overstuffed tradition the lightning is as loud as the bombs.
hope I see your predatory heart it still wants. something
to lose when we look back. on the balcony over the Ministry
of Defence talking about Kafka spare this for me in our
incandescence. there's another reality realty outside pain
as an endless estate hope a body of any other property my
heart is endless darling the next hour is. as inconceivable
as the last still glimpsing. discoveries of the you I
shouldn't have. to say it. not all hope is the same

Dear Lettera 32,
I'm finding it hard to speak I misspell innocence as
oxen eyes see blamelessness in the femme eyes of cows I
think of this alphabetic insight till it recurs I mistype
reference as egg wrench perhaps hope is not anatreptic
seeking out the sweet scent of jasmine flowers at night
I'm still trying not to live like a stray to reply to
each message in a timely manner I don't know how to face
his name when he shoots me in the head in my dreams again
hope the hunting rifle he holds in his hands the next day
I receive a text that says "we will be renaming some sweet
corn plants after you" I know I live on the edge of
mercy another object to sink into there is no abstract
character metaphor or instruction here the carriage
returns aimless notation in each variable line safety is
a kind of thinking where all the tender hearts beep as one

Dear Lettera 32,
I dance when I believe no one else is watching the sea.
eagles the summer the empty campus, even if it means.
getting bitten the bats come out, between the bluish.
accomodation hope behind eyes this unmasked part of me "I
do a lot of different shit but I call it poetry" Johanna
Hedva May 22nd I send my partner a yellow ribbon wrapped
emoji see my digital heart digibanked affection space there
will always be so much left to settle, hope put your
seatbelt on we're going nowhere I didn't notice, the
rotting ceiling tifl I was sitting under if there are a
million interiors of femme, realness pain like hope is
made of mischief I, think I, may never truly decipher.
coconuts bananas or any other mongrel fruit the elegy the
epitaph each typewritten letter I have reassigned, my own
sex hope washed. through the drawn out sky marking out the
way to clarity

Dear Lettera 32,
I know it's out, there an only me that's almost you.hope.
impelled exchange.I swear, it was only half a moon.two
days ago and now it's a whole thing.in sickness,and infirm
delight each, key a hammer hit a bodymaking whole.I move
for, the fifth time.in eighteen months this intrinsic
departure.to safety.I miss home I don't. miss the way, it
tastes under a plane's half shadow.fast moving in flight I
can't. talk about hope as though it's.still happening in
the abundance of softness that comes.in proximity.to fear
"I don't know if I've expressed myself I've probably.
forgotten half the things I wanted to say" Ariana Reines
May 26th.writing at the deterrent.edge of the night I keep.
the windows open to exit completely mellifluous from my
heart its deepest beeps

Dear Lettera 32,

is this a monument I'm writing, to you engraving swift
moments in time. I knew I'd do it. again slowly backwards
drifting it. still all sounds. like bliss we say hope and
do not repatriate growing out of shared thought in love
and writing. I dry tulips by the typewriter every last
place of pollen on grief and stasis. empty the energy of
endless sunrise at the end. of the page this time writing
is recirculating. a slant of elegaic love and letters I'll
wear out. every desire across the epitaph go on it's all
itself again. from hope I want only the beginning

References

Page 6
- "sorrow and rage are appropriate" Ariana Reines
May 19 5:05am, Instagram Live (2020).

Page 11
- "I've said my prayer, I'm not gonna pontificate" Ariana
Reines June 2, Instagram Live (2020).
- "the construction of white innocence indeed" Ariana
Reines June 4, Instagram Live (2020).

Page 18
- "As for we who love to be astonished, the night is lit."
My Life, Lyn Hejinian (1980), pg 68

Page 25
- Feelin' Lovely, Connan Mockasin and Devonté Hynes,
from Myths 001 (2015).
- "let's try and be American just for the hell of it" Ariana
Reines June 4th, Instagram Live (2020).

Page 28
- "I think all my work is pretty pathetic" Eileen Myles
November 11th, Instagram Live (2020).
- "all my poems are pathetic" Eileen Myles November
11th, Instagram Live (2020).

Page 29
- "what if people spy on you in your dreams by dream-
ing themselves into them?" Alice Notley November
25th, Instagram Post (2020) https://www.instagram.
com/p/CIAk8gyBYu1/?hl=en.

Page 32
- "when I do this it's often about my own accountability"
Ariana Reines November 13th, Instagram Live (2020).

Page 34
- "kinship and solidarity and that is why I write" Jordan Scott October 21st, Interview with Broc Rossell (2020).

Page 35
- "voices, weave intimacy, transcendence" Danielle Vogel November 22nd, Vocarium Reading Series: M. NourbeSe Philip & Cecilia Vicuña, from Danielle Vogel to Everyone, Zoom Chat (2020).

Page 36
- "Longing, we say, because desire is full of endless distances." 'Meditation at Lagunitas' from Praise, Robert Hass (1979) https://www.poetryfoundation.org/po-ems/47553/meditation-at-lagunitas.

Page 37
- "write a spell - I will know if it's working" Robert Majzels September 16th, Interview with Broc Rossell (2020).
- "can one take captives by writing, the "one" (first) is "I".", *The Language Of Inquiry*, Lyn Hejinian (2000), pg 62.

Page 38
- "But night, the reserved, the reticent, gives more than it takes.", 'As One Put Drunk Into the Packet-Boat' from *Self-Portrait in a Convex Mirror*, John Ashbery (1975), pg 2.
- "I have no place to take myself except painting", Miyoko Ito, https://youtu.be/UNYcC4WvqO4?t=315.
- "I don't know if what goes on inside me deserves to be called thinking" Gunnar Wærness November 28th, Night and Refuge (2020), https://www.youtube.com/watch?v=IGjDld-PEcQ&t=1434s&ab_channel=caro-linebergvall.

Page 43
- "maybe I don't understand all the languages that address my body" Erín Moure November 28th, Night and Refuge (2020), https://www.youtube.com/watch?v=IGjDld-PEcQ&t=1434s&ab_channel=carolinebergvall.
- "Not that I think it would surprise you. Everyday I see the unbearable beauty and sanity of your eyes, which know everything about me." Two Years With Franz, Franz Wright (2018), https://transom.org/wp-content/uploads/2018/06/Two-Years-With-Franz_Transcript.pdf and https://www.kcrw.com/culture/shows/the-organist/two-years-with-franz.

Page 47
- "every sound we make is a bit of autobiography", 'The Gender of Sound' from Glass, Irony and God, Anne Carson, pg 130.
- "Please let me know if this reached you. I will not intrude on your life in any way. But I miss you so much." Franz Wright, Two Years With Franz, https://transom.org/wp-content/uploads/2018/06/Two-Years-With-Franz_Transcript.pdf and https://www.kcrw.com/culture/shows/the-organist/two-years-with-franz.

Page 44
- "in writing my gender becomes genre", 'Lectures I Will Never Give' from Madness, Rack and Honey: Collected Lectures, Mary Reufle (2012), pg 289.

Page 45
- "the coloured light of a dimension not yet arrived", 'Hello, the Roses', from Hello, the Roses, Mei-Mei Berssenbrugge (2013), pg 61, https://www.poetryfoundation.org/poems/58186/hello-the-roses.

Page 50
- "I like the art of poetry precisely" Ariana Reines

December 7th, Instagram Live (2020).

Page 58
- "talking about the sublime doesn't make it sublime" Khaled Hakim December 23rd, Angels & Daemons: Writing the Mystical with Khaled Nurul Hakim, Rebecca Tamás & Luke Kennard hosted by Penned in the Margins, (2020) https://www.eventbrite.co.uk/e/angels-and-daemons-writing-the-mystical-ticets-132070673941.

Page 63
- Theodore Hopf is fired from NUS the National University of Singapore on December 1st, Jolene Ang (2020), https://www.straitstimes.com/singapore/parenting-education/nus-political-science-professor-dismissed-for-alleged-misconduct.

Page 66
- "encomium – an ancient term for a flattering speech – is an anagram of meconium – the shit we are full of at birth" Anne Boyer December 21st, Substack (2020), https://anneboyer.substack.com/p/the-excremental-ists#:~:text=Unsurprisingly%2C%20encomium%20%E2%80%94%20an%20ancient%20term,was%20the%20attendant%20of%20turds.

Page 70
- "that's what people with stable jobs do is try not to be a menace to society" Ariana Reines December 26th, Instagram Live (2020).

Page 76
- "The screen can be taken away from the fire as long as someone is sitting in the room", *My Life*, Lyn Hejinian (2000), pg 68.

Page 84
- "reality gets jostled and something is opened in that process" Jackie Wang, Hopscotch Reading with Cassandra Troyan & Jackie Wang (2020), https://www.facebook.com/events/d41d8cd9/hopscotch-reading-with-cassandra-troyan-jackie-wang/3554348817988035/.

Page 89
- "language is what makes the wounds come open again", *Plainwater: Essays and Poetry*, Anne Carson (1995), pg 232.

Page 91
- "the problem of the poet is the problem of the life in nerves" Peter Gizzi February 3rd, CITY LIGHTS LIVE! Peter Gizzi in conversation with CA Conrad, (2021), https://www.youtube.com/watch?v=lcksbftcd4Y&ab_channel=CityLightsBooks.

Page 92
- "In the absence of reliable ghosts I made an aria", 'Birthplace with Buried Stones', from *Birthplace with Buried Stones*, Meena Alexander (2013), pg 86, https://www.poetryfoundation.org/poems/56912/birthplace-with-buried-stones.

Page 93
- "if I suffered what else would I do" Bernadette Mayer February 20th, A reading with Bernadette Mayer (2021), https://www.facebook.com/events/d41d8cd9/a-reading-with-bernadette-mayer/885061465562437/.

Page 94
- "I'm not trying to be charming... Poetry proves me. I don't give a shit what happens now", *For Now*, Eileen Myles (2020), pg 46 and 48.

Page 95
- "Will you? Will you?" Alice Notley March 8th, Instagram Post, (2021), https://www.instagram.com/p/CMEtuOZBO2c/?hl=en.

Page 97
- "to write of death is to write of everyone", *The Undying: Pain, Vulnerability, Mortality, Medicine, Art, Time, Dreams, Data, Exhaustion, Cancer, and Care*, Anne Boyer (2019), pg 10.
- "you deserve the peace of living and life" Sonia Sanchez March 26th, Vocarium Reading Series: Tongo Eisen-Martin & Sonia Sanchez (2021), https://www.youtube.com/watch?v=2Iw40TK4tZc&ab_channel=WoodberryPoetryRoom.

Page 100
- "I do a lot of different shit but I call it poetry" Johanna Hedva May 22nd, INVISIBLE COLLEGE presents SNAKE OIL 2021: A CONVERSATION with ARIANA REINES & JOHANNA HEDVA (2021).

Page 101
- "I don't know if I've expressed myself I've probably forgotten half the things I wanted to say" Ariana Reines May 26th, Instagram Live (2021).

"Cat Chong" " In Conversation" "With" "JD Howse"

JH: I wanted to start by talking about the concept of a work being finished. While you were writing Dear Lettera 32, you 'finished' the text on three different occasions, only to feel compelled to pick it up again and add more to it; this is how we ended up having the work in four sections, each section break represents a failed attempt to finish the poem. It was something we spoke about a lot while you were in the process of composing Dear Lettera, with you asking me how you would know when the work was finished, a question I was never really able to answer. I remember sending you pages from Parallel Movement of the Hands, John Ashbery's posthumous collection of 'unfinished longer works' and particularly the quotation 'I am disturbed that it's incomplete, but maybe that's good.'

I wonder if you could talk about your relationship with finality and the text's relationship with finality? Dear Lettera 32 is now being published as a book, but why did you feel the end of the fourth section was the correct place to conclude it, and do you think a work so deeply involved with themes of trauma, pain, and hurt can ever truly conclude?

CC: In Parallel Movement of the Hands, Ben Lerner talks about Ashbery's book as '"hymn to possibility," to borrow a phrase Ashbery used when reviewing Gertrude Stein in 1957, a hymn to ongoingness' which is to say that I think this book's publication as a material object finishes the poem off. Throughout the process I kept being told the project wasn't over and even now I don't think it's done, but I wanted to write through the specific violences I/we were encountering till it felt easier to breathe; I realise I've probably failed any kind of resolute affective valences but I think the desire to stop falling like the wounded in the direction of their wound (to borrow Denise Riley) was, in some sense, concluded, even if the traces of those impacts vibrate way beyond the end of the text; really, I don't know if it's going to feel finished till it's gone.

JH: The subject matter of Dear Lettera 32 is deeply personal but you approach it with a wonderfully analytic and theoretical eye that allows what would otherwise be a closed text to open up into something much more ambiguous. What is your relationship to ambiguity and nuance, and how did you try to navigate the idea of writing the possibility of openness and difficulty into such a personal text?

CC: I think I wanted to keep track of that kind of transmutation into language, into the analogue, or even within the process of the digital. It felt like a process of figuring out how the structures worked. The surface of the digital and of the typewriter held so much in common while remaining vastly different machines which both engaged with the linear shattering of time which occurs under conditions of trauma and distress. I think they both have a fascinating relationship to language as a form of memory. I'd never actually touched a typewriter before starting the project in 2020, I didn't realise the paper wasn't meant to endlessly coil around the carriage, I think some of that openness came from not being able to see more than one line that had been written on the paper so by the time I ran out of space, what unfurled was a very lucid encounter of isolation, grief, desire, and longing for an elseness. There's a very, what I think, amusing oscillation between a lyric I and a consultation of the typewriter manual to figure out what its parts are called, how it comes apart, how to change the ribbons, and so on.

JH: You use the typewriter as a proxy figure in the book; it becomes audience and author, context and subject. At times 'Dear Lettera 32' is very directly standing in for 'Dear [Various Unnamed Real-World Figures]'. It seems to me that whenever you decide to use a specific theme or structure or conceit in your writing, you do it with such multiplicity and in so many different ways, that any divide between the personal and the critical begins to break down. I wonder if this is an expression of your engagement with crip theory and how trauma [physical, medical, emotional, etc] can permeate every aspect of a life?

CC: At first the typewriter wasn't mine; the address of an [Unnamed Real-World Figure] felt true as the machine was something borrowed which is why one appears as a gift at the end of the second section. I think the lack of critical/creative boundaries definitely does emerge out of the academic work I've tried to engage with on crip theory, queer studies, and medical humanities - by the time I was introduced to ideas around disability, gender, and genre I was already chronically ill and trying to figure out how to make undiagnosed chronic pain habitable amongst hostile medical and social institutions. Living inside the theory was something I could intimately feel. I think the multiplicity comes from the "theory" as much as there is any real divide, being at the end of our fingertips. Be it phenomenological or structural, pain is perceived in the body.

JH: and pain is perceived in the page too, visually Dear Lettera is a 'difficult' text in the way the words bunch up and blur together. Obviously this is illustrative of a learning process; of you learning to play the typewriter like an instrument, but I feel like there's a lot more you're achieving with the scripto-visuality of the work (to borrow a term from Redell Olsen.)

CC: You're right about the acoustic learning curve of the typewriter, and a large part of its density owes to kHarLaMoV's aNkLe: A Utopian Fantasy by Robert Majzels, which is one long prose sequence broken only by full stops. It's a spell, there's even a hex at its heart. It taught me how to write out of the kind of captivity pain, lockdown, and grief had given me, to occupy a counter-universe, an anti-gravity. I acknowledge that it's a difficult script to read normatively, but I think that allows it to hold a capacity for being read slant, to encounter the text by cluster, or by verticality rather than in order from left to right.

JH: Could you talk some more about people who influenced the text? Dear Lettera 32 is part of a canon of disabled poets composing on typewriters and incorporating the field of composition into the text itself; I know you and I are both fans of Hannah Weiner and Larry Eigner. The actual work is very intertextual, and incorporates your voracious consumption of poetry and theory directly into itself.

CC: I know we've talked about it a lot, about the relation between disability, language, and the process of writing. We've spoken at length about what an intersectional crip poetics might look like for us now, and about what accessible, liberatory, and joyful practices of composition, editing, and publishing can be. The list of tutelary spirits is long, Hannah Weiner, Bernadette Mayer, Anne Boyer (who's Pulitzer winning book you very kindly gifted to me), Abi Palmer, to name a few, all let the practice of writing infuse the writing. I think it was March 18th 2021 when you sent me that gorgeous quote from page 132 of the Studying Hunger Journals; 'Laugh because now I'm up to the typewriter dream where the whole set of keys come out as if in a drawer, the mechanisms are up above and you know I want a type-writer like this to fill my whole mouth up, the machine's workings a giant sculpture, separate from the keys, a work to observe, it will intensify thought. [...] "Your name is written on it."' She was right about the percolation of thought moving through the instrument and the visceral dimensions accessible through the typewriter which hover over the field of language.

I'm glad the publication preserves the original, hand-done typesetting as well as including the quotations section at the back, as you wrote recently: 'I would like / to be as truthful / as possible'. As the typewriter is such an acoustic machine the writing process felt more like an act of listening, to the keys, to the sounds coming off the screen in lockdown, to the language being put into the air around me. These are my vibrations.

JD: There's an interesting juxtaposition in the text between the presence of the typewriter, the influence of all these poets we love from the 70's, placed against the omnipresent hypermodernity of social media. A lot of the references in the text are to livestreams on instagram, zoom, etc. It reminds me of Lana Del Rey ending her song The Greatest, which is full of personal and cultural nostalgia, with the lyric 'oh, the livestream's almost on' and singing it almost like a sigh, like 'this is what reality has been replaced with.' What role does social media play in the book and how do you reconcile this with the analogue?

CC: I think the typewriter and the phone often feel like a juxtaposition because of their mechanical differences when they're both still on the same continuum - our phones make the sound of hand-typed text and like the poets we love, watching poets over Zoom and Instagram Live is another way of being in the room together. I know it's not the same as name-dropping an exhibition, painting, or sculpture like O'Hara, musicians or poets like Hannah Weiner, or the artists (and their cats) that we count among our friends, as often revolutionary and communal as these acts are, but language has found ways of travelling through the air. Perhaps just as the typewritten text can be felt through the page our machines are connected even just by the practice of listening. We recently went to a podcast recording of an interview with Dionne Brand together, and when she said 'I want accompaniment' it felt true of our instruments of recording, be it our keyboards, touchscreens, or typewriters. I wanted to think through the shared musicality of our linguistic instruments, the percussive indentations of the keys against the carriage and the music emanating from the electrics.

JD: One of the quotes in the book I'm most struck by is the way that 'is this a poem I'm writing to you' transforms into 'is this a monument I'm building to you.' I think something that links our work is this paradoxical fascination with and ambivalence towards form, structure, genre, etc; I think we're both obsessed with understanding the rules of these things, but only so we can understand how to break, alter, ignore, and subvert them. Dear Lettera 32 might be a poem, but it might be a collection of letters, a diary, an epistolary novel, a work of autobiography. What are your thoughts on how others might attempt to categorise the text?

CC: Can I ask you something here? Does Dear Lettera 32 feel like a retaliation? I'm not sure what genre that might be or whether hope, longing, desire, or survival have a default structure, but I've been working on genre theory for a while and I'm starting to think that a part of the ambivalence may be an apathy towards taxonomic legibility. For whom are the categories observed? This is to say, maybe it's a badly written novel.

JD: I guess that's what you're doing in the text; challenging the reader about their assumptions of how they will approach it, and in doing so challenging them to think about the subject matter, the events, the poetic persona, etc? It's inviting, but it's also combative. You call it a retaliation, and you've called it a hex before, and it feels like it could be comforting or confronting depending on how it is approached.

This is going to be the first book published by Permeable Barrier, and there's always an anxiety in launching a new press of not knowing where the book is going to go and who, if anyone, it will reach. I think that goes back to where we started, about knowing when the book is finished; is the book finished because it's in the world or is that just another form of beginning, and one that you have less control over. I wonder if we could conclude here by you talking a bit about how you feel about people reading and interpreting your work?

CC: The 'if anyone' as a clause is comforting. I think when she was asked Dionne Brand said that a poem was finished because 'it was'; I know the unsaid hangs over the language like a veil. At the level of interpretation she also acknowledged the universal as a 'very contentious' construct and I think I agree that I'm not writing after an imagined universal reader but engaging in the writing of a collection that is at once deeply personal while maintaining an openness for the resonance of the reader is an interestingly discursive project. Ultimately, the poem was a survival strategy amidst various hostile structures, actions, and entities and engaging in a sense overwhelmed by the reception of the language would be a form of rumination. Thank you for putting this book out, for approaching it with generosity.

JH: Thank you for allowing me to publish it, I hope readers find it as rewarding as a text as I do.

Acknowledgements

Thank you to those who have opened your instruments, machines, spirits, and minds to this project and shared this time with me. To Ain who has been all the way through with me; JD Howse who's given so much to this project, to Briony, Laura, Emma, Reggie who all read early versions of this work, and to Al, Prue, Cassandra, and Kat for all your enthusiasm and support.

Grateful acknowledgement to the editors of The Babel Tower Notice Board, Osmosis Press for publishing extracts from Part 1 of this collection.

My sincerest thanks to JD Howse for typesetting, proofing, and supporting this project from start to finish.

Typeset in 10pt Futura Medium and
14pt, 26pt Impact Regular by JD Howse.
Original typewriter typescripts by Cat Chong.

Cover design by JD Howse.
Calligraphy by Fay Breed.
Cover: Edited detail of *Le Captif* (1891)
by William Adolphe Bougeureau.
Original held in the collection of Toledo Museum of Art:
Toldeo, OH, USA. Public Domain.

001

Published in 2024
by PermeableBarrier PaperBacks, London, UK.

ISBN 978-1-4461-6812-7

Printed and bound by CPI Group (UK) Ltd, Croydon, CR0 4YY

31/01/2024

03683597-0001